WORKBOOK

FOR

MINDSET

THE NEW PSYCHOLOGY OF SUCCESS

By

Carol S. Dweck

Proudly Brought To You By

WRIGHT PUBLISHERS

Table of Contents

HOW TO USE THIS WORKBOOK

This workbook is a model for anyone who wants to have the right mindset to different situations in life.

This is not another book to be read and dropped. It is a template for anyone who would like to progress and change their outlook on life. It comes with different sections to help you understand, appreciate, and put in the effort to get the change that you require. Change requires work and this book has simplified the work in a more relatable way for you to assimilate and make adjustments.

This workbook is different from every other material, strategy, or class you've ever attempted to bring you your desired change because it helps you to make adjustments from the source of change. This is why it is advisable to go over each chapter as many times as you can.

Remember that your mindset has a way it has worked over the years. When you try out what you've read in this book, you may find yourself saying this isn't possible or you slip back into your previous ways. Don't relent and don't give up. Keep progressing and you'll find out you have the right mindset to life as you do so.

INTRODUCTION

Mindset by Carol S. Dweck Ph.D. is aimed at making every individual a better person. To become better begins in the mind and only a proper mindset can help you achieve anything you want to achieve. People who are remarkable in their fields such as Mohammed Ali, Michael Jordan, and many others have said there was nothing special about them but they had the right mindset to life and they worked towards it.

People who have a natural talent aren't different from those who built it. Sometimes, the people who built and trained themselves to have a talent become better than those who were born with it because they constantly train, develop and improve their talent.

If you don't have the right mindset, there are adjustments you can't make in your life, as well as that of your friends, colleagues, subordinates, mentees, and children. This means one life with the right mindset can make all the changes in different people.

It's not an understatement that a simple belief based on your mindset can make your life beautiful. Who you think you are stems from your mindset and the challenges or hindrances you face can be linked to your mindset.

With the information in this book, you can make your life, your relationship, your business or workplace, your home, and your environment a happy and fulfilling one.

Who should use this workbook?

You need to understand that this book isn't meant for a special group of people. It's meant for anyone who wants to live a fulfilling life. Race, gender, socio-economic status, and other factors don't change or affect anything as much as you're open to learning and development.

What's in it and why is it important to me?

This book is a guide for everyone aspiring to become better at what they do. You'll find out that you can change many negative patterns in your life just by using this book. When you use this workbook, you'll find out that many things that you've termed as normal aren't normal and they can be changed.

This book is important because it is a way to make true and lasting change. It isn't a quick fix to change your mindset. Rather, you can see it s a step-by-step guide to help you spot inconsistencies you didn't know about, and it will help you to grow the right mindset you need to make it work.

CHAPTER SUBDIVISIONS

Each chapter is divided into six parts.

1. Summary: this gives you a background to what you'll find in each chapter. It concisely captures what the chapter is about including the stories that would help you understand the chapter properly.
2. Key takeaways from the chapter: this covers the important points you'll learn in each chapter.
3. Lessons: this covers the wisdom points that can help you in different situations in life.
4. Goals: this is what the chapter set out to achieve.
5. Action plans: this is the working out of the goals.
6. Questions: this is to test your knowledge of what you learned in the chapter.

CHAPTER 1: THE MINDSETS

Summary

There's something children understand about life that adults don't understand; you can learn and cultivate skills. Adults have a straight rule to life; people are either talented or not, they can either succeed or fail, and they can be good or bad. To kids, this position can change.

There are two mindsets. The fixed mindset and the growth mindset. With the fixed mindset you'll continually try to prove yourself to everyone, but the growth mindset believes an individual's qualities can be groomed through plans, hard work, and help from other people.

There was nothing special about Tolstoy and Darwin. They were born normal babies with no special qualities. Cindy Sherman didn't pass her photography course but she was known as one of the most important photographers of the twentieth century. Star actress Geraldine Page was once told to stop acting because she didn't have the talent. These people have proven that if you have the passion for a talent, but you aren't the best, you can develop your talent and become better than those born with a talent.

Key takeaways from this chapter

- We all need role models. They serve as a beacon during critical moments when we feel like giving up.
- Skills can be acquired and learned.

- Human nature can be changed just as personalities aren't cast in stone.
- A person may be known to have a certain personality or character trait that makes him qualify for a position, but it is his effort, training, and experience that he will need the rest of the way.
- Your perspective on life is what determines who you'll become.
- A fixed mindset can begin at an early age, and it makes an individual with this mindset always evaluate themselves with the either-or view.
- Your mindset determines your perspective on hard work and risk. People with a growth mindset appreciate hard work and risk. People with a fixed mindset avoid challenges and hard work.

Lessons

- If you put your mind to it, you can change your personality.
- Life isn't black or white. It isn't either-or, it's not this or that.
- You can teach people about mindsets.
- We all sulk at evaluating our abilities. We either overdo it or underdo it.

Goals

- To understand the two types of mindsets.
- To differentiate mindsets.

Action plans

- Understanding the two mindsets
- Differentiating mindsets

Questions

1. What are the differences between the two types of mindsets?
2. Tick the boxes that apply to you

1. There's nothing you can do to change the level of your intelligence	
2. Nothing is static, you can always boost the level of your intelligence	
3. It's easy for you to learn new things but you know it can't help your intelligence	
4. You can change the level of your intelligence substantially	
5. There's little or nothing that can be done to change who you are because of the kind of person you are	
6. It doesn't matter who you are, what matters is that you can change substantially	
7. Deep down, you know that you can't change even if you do things differently.	

8. There are basic things about your personality that can change.	

If you ticked boxes 1, 3, 5, and 7 then you have a fixed mindset. However, if you ticked boxes 2, 4. 6, and 8 then you have a growth mindset.

3. Your nine-year-old son comes to sit with you while you're gardening. He listened to your podcast about the growth mindset and the fixed mindset. Explain what it means, tell him the difference, and how he can grow his mindset.

CHAPTER 2: INSIDE THE MINDSETS

Summary

Life will throw you different kinds of challenges and only a change in mindset will help you when you find yourself in such challenging situations. If you focus solely on getting accepted or validating yourself instead of what you can learn and how to progress in a situation, you'll never really enjoy your life no matter how much you want to or try.

Understanding mindsets require stepping in and out of them (the mindsets). Entering the fixed mindset will help around you or show how smart you are. Entering the changing or growth mindset means nothing else but growth and learning matters.

The reason why we know about Patricia Miranda isn't just because she lost her mom, or she had an unathletic build as a child. It's because she made up her mind to keep going on while putting in more effort to be a wrestler and to top it all, she made up her mind to explore herself by going for challenges and avoiding the norm when her mom died (was enough reason not to think this way). Christopher Reeve pushed himself passed his limit by taking up learning again even when the doctors warned him and were against it. He pushed himself as painfully as it was and made a positive impact on science. Imagine if he didn't push himself, it would slow down progress in research and science which would eventually affect the whole world negatively.

People with a growth mindset will always put in the effort and never skip a step or rush into a reward without putting in the effort. Janet Cooke and Stephen Glass were not ready for this. Janet worked on an amazing article that got her the Pulitzer Prize but the story was a lie. Stephen also had amazing stories, but his sources never existed. They were later stripped of their prize and honor. Their names are synonymous with phony stories.

Anyone with a growth mindset will seek an objective pattern of reasoning. This doesn't happen to someone with a fixed mindset. Loreta only needed to have a growth mindset to understand what was happening to her.

People with a fixed mindset will define you by failure; reject it and define yourself by your learning abilities, and who you will be. Don't let your experiences define you. You can take charge of your experiences and wield them in a way to favor you.

Key takeaways from this chapter
- Focus on learning and letting go instead of proving yourself.
- There are two ways to view ability. There's a changeable ability and a fixed ability.
- A fixed ability constantly needs to be renewed by proving yourself while a changeable ability is focused on development through learning.

- When you can see and understand mindsets, you'll see that you have a choice. There will be no need to focus on your mistakes and shortcoming or dwell in regret. You'll see life through a different view.
- Where you are determines and defines the world around you. For someone who lives in a growth mindset, there's nothing wrong with efforts or having a setback but in the fixed mindset world, efforts and failures are a bad thing.
- Challenges help people with a growth mindset flourish. People with a fixed mindset don't believe they need to work n their abilities. They believe it shows up on its own.
- As people with growth mindsets flourish when they face challenges, so do people with fixed mindsets who thrive in their comfort zone with nothing challenging because a challenge means they wouldn't feel so smart.
- With a growth mindset, you're flexible enough to see through whatever comes your way without staying fixed on the negative by thinking everyone is out to get you.
- Most of the people who stand out have never been predicted to have a bright future by experts. Experts see potential, but they can never see a future. Your future is determined by the effort you put into developing your skills. They didn't see you put in effort so they can't determine what you'll become.
- When you see yourself as better than others, you constantly compare yourself to them and feel the

need to prove or validate yourself. Every unimportant point will be a big deal to you. The truth is you are special in your way, just as every other person is also special in their way.

- If you have a fixed mindset, your self-esteem is based on how successful you are and this means you're better than everyone else, you believe you have a right to insult or abuse anyone and you live like you're the only one who is worthy.
- Failure has been made to be a noun (an identity or who you are) and not just a verb (an action). Although people with a fixed mindset view the world in this manner, it isn't true.
- With a fixed mindset, failure can be so devastating that the individual doesn't recover from it. These people don't try to fix their damage or failure, rather they focus on improving their self-esteem. This they do by finding someone to blame or comparing themselves with other people who are not doing as well as they are.
- For people with a fixed mindset, the reason why people put in the effort is that they don't have the ability or potential because whatever they do will come to them naturally without effort.
- Success is about becoming your best not comparing yourself to others. See failure as an opportunity to learn and not a condemnation.

Lessons

- Getting the finest things in life may not be the answer to what you feel within (depression or sadness). Becoming and staying content in life is your answer, and this comes from a change in mindset.
- A mindset is a belief that's strong enough to change your world and determine your outcome in any situation.
- You can always change your mind. It isn't cast in stone.
- All you'll ever get in life will be a result of your mindset.
- There are no shortcuts to becoming. It takes effort, learning, and persistence. If you do this, you'll be proud of yourself in the end.
- No one, not even an expert or a professional can determine your future. They can't say who you'll be, what you can do, or how far you can go.
- Potential can't become a result in one day. It grows with time.
- Never choose success over growth. It might seem good initially, but it wouldn't help you build your abilities or strength from within.
- You're not better than others. You just have different potentials and strengths from the other people you're comparing yourself to.

- To be special doesn't mean you're superior or better than others. It is not right to think this way because you'll become self-conceited and self-entitled.
- Don't take things too personally. The world doesn't revolve around you.
- Failing comes to all human beings just as success is a human feat and not for special people.
- Playing the blame game is what makes you a failure. This is because your denial will prevent you from learning.

Goals

- To differentiate mindsets
- To gain the right mindset
- To see the difference between special and superior
- To understand success

Action plans

- Differentiating mindsets
- Gaining the right mindset
- Seeing the difference between special and superior
- Understanding Success

Questions

1. Your daughter came home and told you about her twin friends that lost their parents, gambled with all the money, and lost, and they are having bad grades in school. Explain to your daughter the right mindset to have for this.

2. What future do you see for yourself? Which mindset will get you there?
3. Is it possible to stretch beyond your limit? Express yourself in an area where you'll be willing to do this.
4. Why can hard or difficulty be fun?
5. From the answers you ticked, do you think you have a growth or fixed mindset?
6. What differences can you spot to determine if someone has a fixed mindset or a growth mindset? Mention them.
7. Will being ever be better than becoming? Explain the reason for your answer.
8. You're a coach and there's a new student on your soccer team who has a non-athletic body, isn't so good at soccer but is determined to play. What's your view about the student? Can they be helped or would you encourage them to choose another field? What would you do?
9. Read the story of John Enroe and Michael Jordan. Compare and contrast both stories. What lessons would you learn from both men and what advice would you give to anyone who is like Enroe?
10. Why is effort such a challenge and fear for people with a person with a fixed mindset?

CHAPTER 3: THE TRUTH ABOUT ABILITY AND ACCOMPLISHMENT

Summary

Some people view those who have made remarkable discoveries as mad geniuses who spent time alone, who were deep introverts without caring about anyone else or thinking about others to be able to make a difference. However, this isn't usually the case. Making a difference involves having the right mindset and drive.

A good example is Thomas Edison, the man who had many inventions. He was a normal person just like you and me. He had colleagues and support, so he didn't work alone. He knew the importance of his inventions; he knew how to manage the press and he grew to be a genius; he wasn't born as one. It was his determination and mindset that set him apart. When others lived their normal lives, he put effort into learning and traveling through different states to keep learning so he could come up with inventions. His love for learning consumed him. Other people like Darwin, spent years with colleagues and he put the effort into the field to come up with the origin of species while Mozart spent more than a decade before any of his recognized works became popular.

Times of transition can be challenging for people with a fixed mindset because it's a time to unravel who they are and remove their masks. This means winners can be seen as losers and that's threatening to them. People with this mindset will never let this happen.

People with a growth mindset will always make remarkable decisions and impressions. While students with a fixed mindset will do their little bit (which seems like a whole lot to them) in their studies by picking each course and putting in a little bit of work, students with a growth mindset will find the connecting base between courses by searching for the underlying principles and connections. This way, they get higher grades and appear to be smarter than their fixed mindset counterparts. They know how to stay positive in the face of any challenging situation.

There's no one who can't do better than they think they can if they have the right learning attitude, and are taught right. This is what made Jaime Escalante and Benjamin Jimenez teach their students at Garland High School (which was one of the worst schools) calculus and they made it to the top of the national charts in math.

However, there's a difference between the fixed mindset teacher and the growth mindset teacher. Fixed mindset teachers believe they know their students and can predict their intellectual prowess. Students who begin in the high-grade group were there till the end of the school year and students who were in the low-grade group remained there till the end of the year. For growth mindset teachers, their students ended up as high-grade students whether they began the year as high-grade or low-grade students. This is because of the growth mindset teachers taught their students with the knowledge that everyone would improve, and all students could become better at their skills.

Dedication, training, and effort can never be underrated. It is the way Jackson Pollock who had a small talent for art became one of the greatest painters in America in the twentieth century. It is the way Mozart became respected and esteemed in music.

As bad as negative stereotypes are, they don't affect everyone. Those who are deeply affected are the people with a fixed mindset. Positive stereotypes also affect people with a fixed mindset because when they get a positive label, they do all they can to hold on to it and they get scared of losing it. With negative labels, they fear that this label may be their identity.

Key takeaways from this chapter

- When times get tough, people with a fixed mindset crack under pressure. For students with this mindset, their grades drop, and they have everyone except themselves to blame for this.

- Hard transitions can serve as high risk for students with a fixed mindset.

- In times of transition, adolescents with fixed mindsets pull their resources together to protect themselves rather than use them for learning.

- Many adolescents have the low-effort syndrome which is a way for them to establish their freedom from adults; for those with fixed mindsets, these adolescents see it as a way to protect themselves. To them, adults are weighing, judging, and scrutinizing them and what they have, so they use this strategy to prevent adults from doing this to them. However, for students with a growth mindset, it doesn't stop them from making attempts and putting effort into anything they do.

- Putting effort into anything you undertake doesn't make you smart. It shows you're willing to learn, and this will help you get feedback and constructive criticism to help you improve.

- What students with the growth mindset do when they find themselves in a new learning environment is to take charge of their motivation and learning while fixed mindset students put in effort for their studies but if they get poor grades, they decide that the subject wasn't meant for them instead of asking themselves why they have poor grades.

- People with a growth mindset train their minds to find different ways to learn in every situation.

- If you have the right teaching, the right mindset, and the right attitude to learning, then there will be nothing you can't learn because you can do more than you think you can.

- Grades and test scores as well as other measures of achievement are meant to do one thing: they tell you the current position of the student. They don't tell you where the student will be or what the future of the student should be.

- Why will the fixed mindset never be the best for you?

  - Your peak is capped. If the sky is the limit for everyone, a fixed mindset will not take you past where you are due to the fear of failure.

  - This mindset interferes and hinders any thoughts that would try to make you progress and come out of your comfort zone.

  - It makes putting in effort something that should never be tampered with.

  - It leads to inferior learning.

  - With this mindset, you see other people who are trying to help you or offer you advice as being judgmental, so you avoid them.

- With a growth mindset

  - You're open to all forms of learning if it will help you improve.

  - You see people around you as allies who can help you.

- You're open to correction and constructive criticism.

- You're ready to put in the effort and it's easy to come up with a helpful creative strategy in any situation you find yourself.

- You can use your mind properly and not from a negative stereotype.

- Some people are so graceful in a particular area or field that they can do things with a natural ability. This doesn't mean that others who weren't born with such natural and graceful abilities can't do the same. It only takes training and effort to be as good or even better than people with a natural talent.

- To be creative and excel at anything you do, you need to put in the effort and be dedicated to it.

- First impressions don't last long because they can be changed.

- Stereotypes are terrible because they fill you with thoughts that validate the stereotype.

Lessons

- If two things make the difference in any individual, it's got to be mindset and drive.

- Constantly blaming everyone for the problem will never lead to a solution or show you the way to achieve success in the future.

- Working hard or putting in effort doesn't make you vulnerable.

- Everyone has an interest that can be groomed into an ability.

- A fixed mindset will always hinder achievement.

- Training is important for everyone. It can make you become the best, even better than people who have a natural ability in that field.

- Anything is possible when you're ready to learn.

- Your early performance isn't an indication of your future or talent. It doesn't matter if you start small or poorly. You can learn and train your way up to the top.

- You can become a natural genius if you want to as long as you're ready to learn.

- You must be ready to spend time thinking and building yourself on anything you love. This is called dedication.

- Stereotypes have a way of drawing a person's attention from important things to other distracting things and worries that will confirm the stereotype.

- Girls trust easily and they are easily affected by what other people say or think of them.

Goals

- To understand why you don't need a fixed mindset.

- To embrace the growth mindset

- To grow your mindset

Action plans

- Understanding why you don't need a fixed mindset.

- Embracing the growth mindset

- Growing your mindset

Questions

1. Why do you think some people can achieve more than expected while some achieve less than expected?

2. What's the difference between a fixed mindset teacher and a growth mindset teacher?

3. What is wrong with stereotypes?

CHAPTER 4: SPORTS: THE MINDSET OF A CHAMPION

Summary

No matter how good you are, you can't excel without the mindset of a champion.

People with a fixed mindset have a problem with failure. They always expect to win so when failure happens, they don't know how to manage it. This happens because people with a fixed mindset believe that failure wouldn't happen to them. After all, you've got natural talent.

Let's explain this with an example.

Billy Beane, like people with a fixed mindset, never believed in the effort because he had a natural talent that required no effort. However, natural talent can't take the place of determination and effort. Mohammed Ali couldn't meet up with the physical standard of a boxer. He had neither the chest expansion, nor the fighter's fist, nor the weight, nor reach, nor the physique of a fighter, nor the classic moves, nor the strength. He had nothing except great speed and his sharp mind, so he was wrong for boxing. He sized up his opponent Liston mentally to have an idea of how his mind worked, and Ali used it against him. Ali was a paradox in boxing, but he believed all victories were won from the mind, not from the fists.

It was the same thing that helped Michael Jordan.

He knew that mental strength and heart will always outweigh any physical attribute from opponents. Jordan will tell you that's the reason behind his victories, but many people believe that it was his physical features that made him great.

For Babe Ruth, it was his discipline and constant practice. He committed himself to lose weight and staying fit instead of complaining about how inconsistent his hits were or blaming it on his huge appetite. He loved to practice, and he was resented by his team members for his constant batting practice. Eventually, he was able to give one of the best baseballs hits the world had ever seen.

Wilma Rudolph who was the fastest woman on earth based on her sprint and relay in the 1960 Rome Olympics should never have been the woman with that record. Her childhood made sure of that as she was constantly sick, and she almost lost her life due to a different illness. She had to use a leg brace till she was 12. When she began to run as an adult, she constantly finished last for a long while but with constant practice, and after more losses, she finally began to win. Her last two medals came amid a painful and severe hamstring injury as well as an asthma attack, but she wasn't deterred because she had the mindset that ensured she won.

Experts and professionals know the power of the mind and how it is the essential ingredient that makes the difference but they still publicly declare that it is an innate ability that makes an individual become a genius.

Character is everything. It is the reason why you have come back from your deepest low and win a game without losing focus or becoming too downcast that you can't get back up. It's the reason why Jackie Joyner-Kersee could get through a race when she had an asthma attack and it's the reason she got a bronze medal through a serious hamstring injury. She had told herself to use her pains as the lift to a grand performance.

You can't afford to think too highly of yourself. If you do, you'll relax, relent, and get into a fixed mindset. This is why you need character as this will help you reach the top and stay there. It's all about getting to the top and staying there.

Key takeaways from this chapter

- The effort isn't for weaklings or less endowed people. Even if you have natural talent, you must put in the effort all the time.
- Don't go after talent or natural abilities. Go after mindset and you'll get the talent.
- Our expectations and reality may clash. There are people with natural talents and physiques who don't go far while those whom we would naturally overlook will far surpass our expectations.
- It is only natural for humans to look at the physique or other physical attributes to make our judgments about who would win in a competition, but it is our minds that make the difference.
- Many of the people we idolize in the world of sports are not born different from us. They weren't born as

extraordinary individuals, rather they built their minds, put in the effort, and went through training.

- Character is what makes you keep going. It is what makes you look deep within and find the strength to go on when the odds are set against you.

- With a fixed mindset, people get buried in their specialness and talent. This makes it difficult to forge ahead when things go wrong. They throw tantrums, lose their ability to progress, blame everyone, and work against everything they previously worked for.

- With the right mindset, you can overcome any challenges or setbacks, find a good strategy to help you cope during a challenge, and act in the best interest of you or your team in any situation.

- People who become champions have character, they put in the effort, they stay focused under pressure no matter the distraction, and they can stretch themselves when they needed to do so.

- Ability and character serve different purposes. While ability gets you to the top, the character will keep you there. With character, you have to work hard or twice as hard to stay on top.

- People with a fixed mindset believe athletes must:
  - Have a certain ability to be a sportsman and there's nothing that can be done to change that.
  - Be naturally gifted. You must have the natural talent to be a sportsman.
  - Succeed by maintaining their superiority.

- Search for their talent and let it carry them through instead of looking for how to improve their abilities.
- Validate their talent.
- People with a growth mindset believe:
  - You can improve at sports when you put in more effort.
  - Learn and practice skills and techniques constantly.
  - In sports, you own the process that brings success and maintain it.
  - With team effort, you can win championships while an individual or superstar wins games.
- There's no need to worry about being a nobody. Focus your energy on using all you've got to deal with the task in front of you.

Lessons

- Failure isn't meant for aliens. It happens to all humans so it can happen to you. This means you need to know how to deal with it.
- A great mind and mindset is the best tool for anyone who wants to excel in their chosen field.
- Success begins in the mind and is followed by determination and effort. No sportsman who has these unique features will regret it.
- Culture talks about the importance of individual effort and the need to improve ourselves but deep down, we don't believe in this. We would rather believe in extraordinarily born beings as the ones

who make the difference. The world doesn't care about hard work and effort but only about professionals. They don't care what it takes to get to the top as long as you're there.

- Without character, effort and hard work would be a waste.
- Mindset is the foundation for character.
- A champion is someone who can win no matter the circumstance. You have the backing of your character to help you gain the strength you need from within. You can raise the level of the game when necessary. When the going gets tough, you can emerge three times tougher.
- The right mindset also includes having a championship mentality. This is what makes you beat your opponent who is better than you. With this mentality, you can rebound from any situation.
- Enjoy the process as well as the results. No part should matter over the other. Both parts account for success.
- Embrace your failures. Don't avoid them.
- The mindset of a champion, heart, and character accounts for great athletes who have a growth mindset that makes them focus on self-motivation, self-development, and taking responsibility.

Goals

- To hear the mindsets of athletes
- Stop worrying and start acting.
- To succeed

- To have the mindset of a champion

Action plans

- Hearing the mindset of athletes
- Stop worrying and start acting.
- Succeeding
- Having the mindset of a champion

Questions

1. Mindset or talent which one would you pick if you had a choice? Explain the reason for your choice.

2. Choose the better answer among the following:

- Mindset vs Talent
- Process vs talent
- Physical endowment vs intellectual endowment
- Mind vs performance
- Natural endowment vs earned ability
- Curiosity vs natural ability
- Character vs talent
- The right mindset vs agility
- To feel special or to work hard.

3. Why do naturals care less about hard work and methods to cope with failure?
4. What makes character important?
5. Where does character come from?
6. How can mindset help people cope with failure, setbacks, and rejection?
7. Do you think a character can be learned? Explain the reason for your answer.

8. What makes a person a champion?
9. What's the benefit of being mentally tough?
10. What people are better at sports and why? Is it the fixed mindset individuals or those with a growth mindset?

CHAPTER 5: BUSINESS: MINDSET AND LEADERSHIP

Summary

In this chapter, we see different leaders, their different mindsets, their leadership strategies, their good deeds, their mistakes, and how they made them thrive or brought their downfall.

A leader is like a driver in a car who determines where the company goes, how fast it grows, and how to sustain it. A leader's attitude and mindset are everything.

Such a leader is objective and proactive. An example of such a leader is Alan Wurtzel, the CEO of Circuit City. He used his board of directors as means of learning which was why he held debates in his boardroom. He used them as a sounding board without thinking of impressing them. His board served as a testing ground where he could test run his idea and try to see from their eyes. This way, he was sure that the ideas he was set to implement will be beneficial to everyone at all levels. He continually held on to any idea he didn't understand until he understood it.

CEOs have so much power that they can either use it to build their need for validation and focus on petty things or they can be objective and focus on what's good for the company.

Albert Dunlap was a CEO who was profit-driven and he cared less about everything else. His way of saving companies was by getting them ready to be sold again and laying off workers. He openly admitted being in business just to make money and when he was asked about making charitable donations, he gave an emphatic no. He was a man focused on proving himself by making money and showing he was a genius. Clearly, employee welfare and charitable deeds were not a part of his standard. He had his chance to make a difference, but he didn't have the right mindset for it. When he took over Sunbeam, he sold major parts of the plants and laid off half of the staff. He couldn't sell the company because the stocks were too expensive so he ran it but he got kicked out. He was found to default on about $1.7 billion loan. He couldn't stand it when the employees spoke back to him or asked questions because he felt superior and entitled.

Ken Lay who believed he was a great visionary, was another CEO who looked down on everyone else. The perception was more important to him than anything else. He always set out as a regal man who wanted everyone to believe he was kind and supportive. That was the impression he wanted people to have especially those on Wall Street even though none of it was true. He met Jeff Skilling, another CEO who intimidated others using his brainpower. Jeff always treated those he felt were beneath him in a harsh manner and anyone who wasn't on his side wasn't bright enough to understand. Skilling always believed he was smart enough to beat the odds.

Another example was with Steve Case and Jerry Levin the CEOs of AOL and Time Warner respectively, who came together but their quest for power and fixed mindsets almost ruined the company. They couldn't run the company together as each of them focused on gaining personal power. Their company eventually fell and was known as the company with the largest annual loss in the history of American business.

Positivity and energy are major hallmarks of companies run by a growth mindset boss. These kinds of bosses know that the best employees have the right mindset, not just the certificates to show for it. This is the kind of boss Jack Welch became at GE. He opened room for dialogue and honest feedback when he became CEO and he made sure everyone saw that the company wasn't about him. It was about growth and not about the CEO. He ensured that leaders shared the credit with their teammates instead of taking the whole credit themselves.

Lou Gerstner was also the CEO of IBM with the right mindset. He worked on opening communication on all grounds (between leaders and subordinates from top to bottom and bottom to top), and he moved among his subordinates to engage them. He dissolved the management committee, canceled the power of the executives, and moved to speak to everyone as long as they had something to offer. He didn't like cliques or politicians, but he loved teamwork and made sure every project and idea was executed. He put the customer first and didn't focus on himself.

It's the same thing that Anne Mulcachy of Xerox did when she took over. She focused on learning so she could become the right person who could lead the company. She was compassionate but tough which is why she cut 30% of employee rolls. To manage this, she moved among the staff and apologized for it. Growth was a drive to her, but she was concerned about her staff. She retained the company culture of celebrating staff so she could save the company.

Men are not the only ones who can be CEOs; women can do this, as they now hold key positions in top companies.

Negotiation is a top skill required for all businesspersons.

Key takeaways from this chapter

- Anyone with a fixed mindset would rather blame than accept and correct their shortcomings. When you put people in an environment that focuses on their innate talent instead of their ability or growth, you're telling them image is everything and they will find it challenging when their image is threatened. They will do everything to protect themselves including lying or taking a shortcut to the end.
- In companies where there are effective leaders, these leaders are remarkable because:
  - They have a growth mindset.
  - They are not trying to outdo themselves.
  - They don't compare themselves to others.
  - They don't always want to take the credit or be at the center of everything.

- o They trust their subordinates and they leave them to manage their affairs.
- o They don't make their subordinates feel small so they can feel big.
- o They aren't threatened by the improvements of others.
- o They always want to improve.
- o They make use of the ablest people around them.
- o They do not shy away from their mistakes and deficiencies.
- o They identify the skills they and the company will need in the future.
- o They work with facts, not fantasies.
- o They are hardworking.
- o They promote growth, creativity, and possibility.
- o They believe in the development and human potential of other people.
- o They walk their talk. They put their talk into action.
- o They believe everyone deserves to be heard.
- o They don't have a larger-than-life mindset.
- o They are kind to the faults of others.

CEOs and leaders with a fixed mindset

- o Can create a world where they only listen to the things that appeal to them.
- o Focus on their perfection and what they are doing right.

- They only see the successful part of their company no matter how loud the warning signs may be.
- Feel entitled.
- They choose to blame others and opt to look good when they have a chance to make important decisions for the good of the company.
- They always lead their companies to the brink of destruction.
- They create their reality and cloak themselves in royalty while looking down on others.
- They encourage group thinking.

- Fixed mindset leaders want to be the only big fish that can't be compared with other people.
- Some CEOs build a gargantuan personal ego so that when they leave, it will quicken the end of the company or keep it mediocre.
- The big egos that CEOs have today can be traced to Iacocca. From his time, CEOs became superheroes who only care about their egos and are less concerned about corporate health. He worked with Henry Ford II and craved the benefits of working with him. He wanted to be the heir to Henry but it didn't happen. Iacocca was a man who did all to protect the company's image but wouldn't work for the benefit of the company. He continued with

Chrysler Motors after Henry Ford ditched him and when Chrysler was going to get bankrupt, he didn't focus on the right things. He worried someone else was going to take the credit for his feats, so he didn't approve of ideas that could save the company. He fired the important subordinates but hung to his title even when he lost his effectiveness. He was a perfect example of a fixed-mindset leader.

- The greatest leaders in the world had nothing to prove. They only did what they did because they loved the work, and they wanted it to progress. This should be the heart of every leader.
- Abusive and controlling bosses force subordinates into a fixed mindset.
- Group thinking can be damaging to a company.
- When people have faith in their leader, it can lead to group thinking.
- Your mindset will influence your negotiation skills. With the right negotiation skills, you can spot and understand the other person's interest. This skill will help you gain a robust outcome for yourself, and you can come up with a creative solution that is beneficial to all parties, not just one person.
- An organization can either be driven by the culture of a genius (fixed mindset) or the culture of development (growth mindset)

Lessons

- A company that can't correct itself can't grow or thrive.

- The greatest leaders have never been people who want to be show-offs. They simply want to do their piece without the spotlight on them.
- The solution to a problem can never be picking out other people's faults. It's in doing your part and getting it right.
- The fact that you're a leader or you're in a privileged position doesn't mean you're better than others and you shouldn't ignore their needs or what they have to say.
- When leaders believe they are superior, they tend to wield power and competence at the expense of their subordinates which makes them brutal bosses.
- Never resort to humiliating your subordinates. It will prevent them from speaking the truth to you which will lead to a stifling, non-creative, and hostile work environment.
- To be truly self-confident requires that you are courageously open, and you're not afraid to accept new ideas irrespective of the source.
- Self-confidence doesn't begin on the outside which covers what you do, how you look, and how expensive you dress. It begins from within.
- If you're focused on growth, ego wouldn't drive you.
- You can be trained on anything. You can be trained to have a growth mindset; you can be trained to be a leader.

Goals

- To gain the right mindset as a leader

- To be the right leader
- To gain negotiation skills

Action plans

- Gaining the right mindset as a leader
- Becoming the right leader
- Gaining negotiation skills

Questions

1. Why does every company need a leader with a growth mindset?
2. Why do companies opt for CEOs who have a larger-than-life mindset about themselves, and they'll focus more on themselves than the company?
3. If you were Iococca what would you have done differently?
4. How can a CEO avoid the CEO disease and the dangers that come with a fixed mindset?
5. Do you think businesses should solely focus on making a profit and nothing else? Explain the reason for your answer.
6. What's the easiest way to become a hostile and horrible boss?
7. What are the causes of group thinking? Should it be encouraged?
8. What are the benefits that come with good negotiation skills?

9. What is wrong with corporate training?
10. What do you need to create a growth mindset environment?
11. Why do employees in growth mindset companies have a positive view?

CHAPTER SIX: RELATIONSHIPS: MINDSETS IN LOVE (OR NOT)

Summary

To become happily ever after with your true love, expect many bumps along the way. These bumps are hewn from heartbreaks, disappointment, frustration, and a lot of bittersweet memories. It's not going to be a smooth and hassle-free journey.

Heartbreaks and rejection mean different things to people, depending on their mindset. If you don't want someone else to be happy because the person broke your heart, it will take more effort from you because it will make you more unhappy.

For people with a growth mindset, everything that happens gives them a reason to learn. Heartbreak and broken relationship are other reasons and ways to learn. These people always take something out which is what they've learned. If you decide to start a pity party for yourself, there will be many things to keep you down. This is what Cousin Cathy understood when she decided to shake herself up from her pity party and go dancing even with her injury. If she didn't go dancing because she was hurt, she would have continued to feel miserable and missed the chance to meet her husband. This was what the Contos family realized when they continued with the party celebrations even after Nicole was no longer getting married. Nicole decided she was going to survive and that's the reason why she got into the press the following day.

A fixed mindset can make relationships burdensome. It's the reason why Charlie couldn't speak to Yvonne when she was running late in picking up the kids, spending more time with her friends, and receiving strange calls. If Charlie confronted her, he would have had to accept that he either married a bad person or he was the bad one who pushed her away or their relationship was a bad thing.

A relationship isn't a competition. No one is giving you a medal for outdoing your partner. Focus on helping your partner grow just as you grow and encourage each other's development.

Your friends are important, and you should keep the right set of friends. Your friends are people who can help you grow, and boost your development just as you do the same for them.

Shy people are afraid to give themselves up or become vulnerable with their friends. They get embarrassed quickly especially when they find themselves in social gatherings because they fear that they'll be embarrassed or judged. This pushes them into anxiety, their heart rate quickens, they avoid eye contact with others, and they give no room for communication and interaction or when it happens they end it abruptly.

Key takeaways from this chapter

- Heartbreaks and disappointments on your way to finding true love will happen. it happens in marriages as well. You just need to make sure the scar is not an indelible mark that prevents you from loving again or giving yourself up for love's sake. Those with a growth mindset, know lack of forgiveness will be a hindrance to love, and rejection is not a permanent thing.

- When they face heartbreak, disappointments, and rejection, people with a fixed mindset believe they are meant to be permanently labeled as unlovable. They don't heal because they don't know how to, and they hurt the other people they got into a relationship with or the people they married. This happened because they held on to their hurts with plans of how to hurt the person who hurt them.

- For people with a growth mindset, the way forward is to understand, hurt, forgive, heal, and move on. For those with a fixed mindset, the way forward is to feel bad about yourself and plot revenge.

- People who are great with interpersonal relationships are gifted.

- Generally, we don't understand that having relationship skills is a special gift, hence our inability to appreciate it. With the help of mindset, we can understand people's skills better.

- We all need to understand mindsets because:

- They help us understand why people don't learn about the skills they need for relationships.
- They help us understand why people have skills but don't use them.
- It helps us to make sense of the reason people give their all in a relationship, yet they always seem to undermine themselves.
- It helps us to see the reasons why love can turn sour.
- With it, we can know why people can build lifelong and fulfilling relationships.

- With a fixed mindset in a relationship, a person believes nothing can change. He believes he's meant to be the way he is, and the same thought goes for his partner and the relationship. He believes the ideal is something you have from the beginning, and so is compatibility. To this person, everything must be perfect from the beginning.
- With a growth mindset in a relationship, a person believes everything needed for the relationship can be developed. You, your partner, and your relationship can grow and develop because there's no one who isn't capable of growth. You live above blaming your partner or anything else.
- The challenges that come with a fixed mindset are
- You don believe in working hard and putting effort into the relationship.
- You expect a perfect relationship from the beginning.
- You believe all the problems will go away on their own.

- It's a fallacy to believe that being in love means everything is magically perfect.

- Relationships and marriage are about two different people coming together. You learn about yourselves by communicating. Couples who grow old together are used to their lifestyles and they didn't begin by reading each other's minds.

- Couples don't need to have each other's views because they are a couple. You don't need to have the same expectations, goals, and aspirations. You're still an individual just as your partner is an individual too.

- With a fixed mindset, you'll assign blame in your relationship, and this is dangerous for any relationship.

- Don't assume that your partner can never change traits or habits. Each person can change, but that doesn't mean they will eventually change.

- Friends are great because you can encourage each other without giving yourselves unnecessary praise, you can encourage yourselves when you need to boldly make decisions that may appear challenging if you're aloof and support each other.

- Bullying is about judging and showing who's important. Their victims are treated with terrible standards not fit for humans. Bullies gain their strength from their actions, by making everyone fear them. Bullies have fixed mindsets. Many of their victims also have a fixed mindset and they eventually become bullies as well but those with the growth mindset eventually get to forgive their bullies.

Lessons

- When you hold on to hurt or refuse to love others, you're hurting yourself more. By blocking out something as good as love, you're making yourself cold to receive and give love.
- Love isn't enough for a relationship because it needs to be supported by effort and a lot of help.
- After a heartbreak, the best place to begin is to understand and forgive.
- We need people around us who are our support system for the good times and (especially) for the bad times.
- Your marriage needs your help to work because the tension and other issues are strong enough to force the relationship apart.
- Whatever you leave to itself without constant care and effort will grow wild. This is one reason why relationships fail.
- Assumptions can hurt relationships. This is why mind-reading doesn't work.
- You and your partner don't have to agree on everything.
- There's nothing perfect in life. Everything great and perfect had a time when there were setbacks.
- There's no one without flaws. You have yours and so does your partner.

- If someone close to you makes you feel small so they can boost their confidence and self-worth, that's not a friend.
- No one deserves to be bullied.

Goals

- To understand why you need to forgive.
- To gain relationship skills
- To see the place of mindset in relationship
- To see the importance of effort in a relationship
- To avoid assumption and mind-reading.
- To build a pattern of communication in marriage
- To understand what friendship entails and know those who are your friends.
- To help shy people.
- To understand the bullying mindset

Action

- Forgiving others
- Gaining the right skills for a relationship
- Seeing mindset and using it well
- Put effort into your relationship so it works
- Avoid assumptions and stop mind-reading.
- Building communication patterns for your marriage
- Understanding friendship
- Know those who are your friends.
- Helping shy people become sociable.
- Understanding the bullying and victim mindset

Questions

1. Why can revenge never be a way out when your relationship fails?
2. Do you think all you need for a relationship is love? Explain the reason for your answer.
3. Why is forgiveness a good thing?
4. What works better in a relationship? Asking questions to gain clarity or reading your partner's mind? Explain the reason for your answer.
5. What are the things that you wouldn't give up because of marriage? List them out. Ask your partner to do likewise and show it to each other.
6. What are the problems associated with having a fixed mindset in a relationship?
7. Is it possible to showcase your skills in a relationship in a non-threatening way?
8. Why is friendship important?
9. Why are people shy? Is shyness a sign of a fixed mindset?

CHAPTER SEVEN: PARENTS, TEACHERS, AND COACHES: WHERE DO MINDSETS COME FROM?

Summary

There's no parent who doesn't want the best for their child and who wouldn't give anything to see their child become the best. However, their action or inactions in this light can boomerang.

The messages you pass to your kids may be from a fixed mindset which tells them you're judging them because they have permanent defects. You may also be sending them a growth mindset message which says that you understand them, you see they are growing and developing, and you're committed to their growth and development.

You may think you're praising, affirming, or validating your kids but this serves as pressure for them. You may be telling your kids, you did so well in that test, you're so brilliant but the kids hear 'if I don't do well in my test, I'm not brilliant'.

Some parents believe in verbally boosting the confidence of their children. This kind of confidence is fleeting and doesn't help the child. Children must learn by themselves to build their confidence. They need to know their capabilities.

As a parent or teacher, don't focus solely on your child or student's intelligence. That's a fixed mindset approach. They are other abilities they can gain by training and learning, so you can focus on these as well. According to Haim Ginott, praise is meant to work on the achievement and effort of your child and not focus on the child's personality.

The perspective of kids with fixed mindsets differs totally from the perspective of the kids with growth mindsets. It doesn't matter if the parents were trying to help them, kids with fixed mindsets saw their parents judging them while kids with growth mindsets saw their parents were trying to help by making corrections.

All that has been said about parents applies to teachers because they spend time shaping their students. They also have to set standards for different students with different backgrounds and challenges from home. They must be able to help their students and set standards that aren't too low for each of them while remaining balanced, empathetic, and objective.

With a fixed mindset, an individual will always remain complicated. This means the person can be nice, friendly, and have other impressive attributes, but you can't trust that the person's ego wouldn't come up at the wrong time. One such person is coach Bobby Knight. Bobby is kind, gracious, caring (especially about his players), cruel, and judgmental.

Coach John Wooden was a growth mindset coach who had one of the best championship records in sports history. He got into UCLA and met inadequate facilities like the poorly ventilated gym. Sometimes he had to borrow a gym from other schools or towns. His players were terrible, but he constantly trained them to become the best. For him, each individual had to put in daily effort so they could become better without passing the message that they couldn't make mistakes. He respected all his players equally with no favorites. Concern, passion, and consideration were his priorities.

A growth mindset is development oriented. It focuses on the growth and development of the people. It doesn't come by speaking positive words but by acting toward them.

Key takeaways from this chapter

- As a parent, teacher, and coach, your actions, words, body language, and inactions, all send a message to your kids, students, and athletes. This is what tells them how you view them and how they are to see themselves.
- Many parents protect their children from failure. While this is okay and can help your child get through what he's feeling it has an adverse effect in the long run. What happens when you're not there with the child?

- Children may say something, but they mean something else. It takes someone with a growth mindset to understand them.
- Praising the intelligence of your kids can hinder their motivation which will affect their performance. Your praise makes them happy for a moment and gives them confidence. After this, their confidence hits a snag and they begin to think that once they don't meet up with your expectation, they have nothing to offer.
- You can't give out permanent confidence to your child. It's not a gift or package you can hand out to them.
- Instead of constantly validating and praising your child, the best thing you can do for them is to bring challenges their way. Let them love learning from mistakes, let them love teamwork, seek out a solution on their own, and love learning.
- There's nothing wrong with praising a child. You only must do it right and this means not praising or focusing on their talent.
- Parents need to know you can't praise your child yet say harsh things to others in their presence. If you do this, it will boomerang on your kids.
- When you focus on the speed and lack of mistakes of your children during any task, you normalize speed and perfection which will make it difficult for your children to persevere when they are faced with any form of challenge.

- Kids with a fixed mindset believe their parents judge them because of the kind of messages they get from them. Kids with a growth mindset believe their parents encourage them to learn and pick up good habits from them because of the kind of messages they receive from them.
- Children are natural teachers. They'll always pass on what they learn. If they receive judgment and abuse from home, they'll pass it on to their peers. If they receive love, correction, and encouragement, they'll pass it on to their peers.
- When you judge and punish your child, you're telling them not to think through their issues but to always protect themselves by any means instead of owning up to what they did wrong and finding a way out through a challenge.
- Both fixed mindset and growth mindset parents set high standards for their children. The difference is that growth mindset parents show their children ways to meet the standard while fixed mindset parents expect that their children reach their standard on their own. When they proffer help, fixed mindset parents do it through judgment, punishment, and labeling their children.
- John McEnroe's father was judgmental and loved his son on his terms. The older McEnroe made sure his son succeeded yet John never liked it. This is different from Tiger Woods's father who made sure his son focused on growth and learning while nurturing the boy's love for golf.

- If you don't have a passion for teaching and you're not willing or ready to put in the effort to learn, research, and learn about children, don't attempt to venture into teaching. It takes teachers like Marva Collins, Rafe Esquith, and Dorothy DeLay who could see, understand, and help their students who are at the low-end to get to become a high-grade students. Sometimes, it only takes the love of learning and the children to push you on when you're tired or you feel like giving up.
- With the challenge and nurture approach, you can never go wrong as a teacher. It takes a teacher showing the student that the school (and the teacher especially) is there to ensure that their minds grow.
- A fixed mindset teacher believes that their role is simply to impart knowledge to their students. They believe they don't need to gain more knowledge and their students know their classes will always be boring.

Lessons

- Good intentions may not always yield the best result.
- Children take your messages seriously. They are sensitive to it.
- As a parent, you must live out what you say especially for the sake of your child.

- An individual's achievement and skills will be a result of how much effort and commitment they give.
- Mistakes are a part of your child's growing process. Help them see that.
- Constructive criticism is meant to help a child, student, or athlete. Don't withhold it from them.
- All kids misbehave at some point.
- From a young age, parents pass the message that their kid's mistakes are worthy of judgment and punishment.
- Children cry. They cry because they have a need that needs to be met.
- Being a growth-minded parent doesn't mean you pamper and indulge your child.
- As a parent, you don't have to love your child on your terms. You aren't the center of your child's world and your child doesn't live for you. Don't make your child live to please you.
- When parents set ideals for their kids, they need to know if the ideals are helpful or not. Don't make your child into the carbon copy of your dreams and validate them based on this.
- It is always difficult when you know that your colleagues know something and you are the only one who is struggling with it. This is even more difficult for students who usually feel the gap is unbridgeable.

Goals

- To see the effect of praising your child
- Stop praising your child for their talent
- To create new strategies to help your child.
- To normalize challenges for your child
- To teach your child to have a love for learning.
- To teach your child to be creative
- To help your child see the benefit of team effort.
- To know how to reassure your child
- To know how to criticize your child constructively.

Action plans

- Seeing the effect of praising your child.
- Stop praising your child for their talent.
- Creating new strategies to help your child
- Normalizing challenges to your child.
- Teaching your child to have a love for learning
- Teaching your child to be creative
- Helping your child see the benefit of team effort
- Knowing how to reassure your child
- Criticizing your child constructively

Questions

1. What effect does praise have on a child?
2. What's the best gift a parent can give to a child?
3. What is wrong with handing down confidence to your child?

4. Your daughter wants to join the science club but she feels it might be too difficult so she's thinking of opting out. What can you tell her?

5. Your teenage nephew said his younger half-brother is taking piano lessons. No one is encouraging him, but your nephew wants to do this. He doesn't know the right way to go about it since his half-brother isn't so good and he doesn't want to lie to his brother. What can he say to him?

6. Should you reassure your child before a test? Explain the reason for your answer.

7. Sandy who is your neighbor's daughter is good at gymnastics. She's going to a competition, and she tells you confidently that she's going to win a prize. She does her part well during the competition, but she doesn't win, and she is depressed. What would you tell her afterward?

8. How can you differentiate between constructive criticism and judgmental criticism? Explain using examples.

9. Your child would rather play games than study. You've always told him to stop it and concentrate. At the end of the school term, he has a bad grade. You're upset and frustrated. What is the right way to express your frustration to him?

10. What's the difference between a growth mindset parent and a fixed mindset parent?

11. What misunderstandings do people have about the growth mindset?

12. How can you pass on a growth mindset to your kids?

CHAPTER EIGHT: CHANGING MINDSETS

Summary

In this chapter, we see kids and adults who made the change using their abilities and how everyone can do the same.

Change is hard for everyone especially kids. It comes with a feeling of helplessness for them and it's worse if they have fixed mindsets. If a child is content and happy in a school, and there's a reason to change homes or environment, it can be scary for kids which brings with it a feeling of hopelessness.

Change doesn't mean removing batteries from a remote or any other device. It isn't replacing your mindset at the snap of your fingers. Rather, it's a whole lot of work. It is having a new reference apart from your old mindset and you have the option to choose from there.

The mindset you have is what guides your belief and interpretation. When you have a growth mindset, it can lead to a change in your perception and the way you relate with everyone around you. It changes your mindset from protecting yourself and your ego to becoming more open to change and taking risks.

Cognitive therapy is important. This is because it helps people to think more realistically and make optimistic opinions and judgments.

When you tell people to give up or change their mindset, you're telling them to change themselves because this is who they have been for a long time. It's difficult so you need to be empathic.

Children love the fixed mindset because it fills them with the idea of being worthy, succeeding, and being the adulation of everyone. It makes them feel like a star.

When trying to make changes and you turn to willpower, understand that it isn't enough. Willpower works with strategies, not from thinking about stopping a habit or changing a routine to make things work out for you.

The things you consider the best or finest things in life may not have the same meaning to your children. If you choose one of the best schools for your children or one of the best tutors for your children, it may be putting them under a lot of pressure. You may be thinking 'I'm doing the best for my kids. They are lucky because I didn't have this when I was their age'. Guess what? Your child may be thinking 'I mustn't fail mum' instead of focusing on learning, growth, and enjoying her life.

Key takeaways from this chapter
- For children with fixed mindsets, when change comes, they feel incapable and powerless.

- When you decide to make a change in your mindset, you are telling your mind to choose from another option. This can be difficult but the more you use this, the more this reference becomes stronger.

- Beliefs give us a reason to be either happy or sad. Our minds can either be consciously or subconsciously aware of it. It is the reason why we interpret situations and the feelings that come with them the way we do. The framework of your belief is provided by your mindset.

- The fixed mindset is set on the judgment which brings labels such as 'I'm a loser', or 'I'm a terrible person'. People with this mindset are sensitive to words and they classify words under a positive or negative label.

- The internal monologue of people with a growth mindset is focused on constructive action and learning. This doesn't mean they aren't also sensitive to the words spoken to them, it only means their focus isn't on classifying this information as being judgmental. They would rather focus on 'how do I become better' or 'how can I help others become better?'

- As great as cognitive therapy is, there are things beyond its power:
  o it can't take away a fixed mindset.
  o It changes the judgmental lens and ears that people with a fixed mindset use.
  o It can't take the focus away from being judgmental.
  o It can bring a growth mindset.

- The fact that you have a growth mindset doesn't mean you're immune to disappointments or hindrances. It only means you're not resolved to think or live in that way. You'll live your life without focusing on setbacks or judgments.
- People who hold on to a fixed mindset have their reasons (even if they think it's a crazy idea), and their reasons are sensible.
  - It might be that it gave them a view of life.
  - It can be the reason some people know how to behave in public or when they are away from home.
  - It could have given people a way to find themselves.
  - It could have helped them grow their self-esteem.
  - For some children, it was the reason they felt loved (and children will give up anything to feel this way) or this was the way to be noticed by a parent, a teacher, or an important adult in their lives.
  - It offered a straight way to life. There was no need to think of other possibilities.
- A growth mindset doesn't prevent you from having quarrels or disputes with others. It only helps you to move on quickly without bitterness, judgments, or any negative emotion that can hinder your progress. You'll find yourself moving with understanding and new skills for problem-solving.
- There's nothing easy about change, especially mindset change. If you find yourself going back to the previous way you used to think, don't be discouraged or blame yourself. Identify what went

wrong and move on with the new mindset you've come to embrace.

- People with a fixed mindset
  o Have an entitlement mentality.
  o They believe the world needs to change and not them.
  o They don't like challenges or disagreements or problems; they'll rather run from them. They'll take pseudo-peace over confrontations or arguments with others.
- When you are growth minded at work, you'll notice
  o Spending time with your colleagues is a good idea because it helps you build relationships.
  o You can help your colleagues grow and develop.
  o It brings satisfaction and you're at peace with yourself.
  o People will help you and support you.
  o Everyone around you is no longer an adversary plotting your downfall or judging you.
- To help kids with a fixed mindset, encourage them to
  o Talk about the ways they made friends with others.
  o To stop talking about their abilities.
  o To stop comparing themselves with others.
  o To help others.
  o To communicate with others clearly.
  o To play with others and not stay aloof.
- When you are making a change in your lifestyle and you begin to get better, don't stop what you're doing that brought about the change. Changes don't

implement themselves, and they stop when you stop what you're doing to improve.

- To change from a fixed mindset
- Accept that you have a fixed mindset.
- Know the triggers and know your persona.
- Know what happens after it is triggered.
- Expect setbacks.
- Don't compare yourself to someone else. Don't judge yourself. Just observe.
- Your fixed mindset needs an identity. Name it.
- Teach your fixed mindset persona the growth mindset.
- Don't avoid this persona and don't act like you're above it already because it doesn't disappear.
- Create strategies and set goals to help you manage the fixed mindset.
- Always keep your growth mindset in your thoughts.

Lessons

- Whatever you give power to or whatever reference you use will become stronger as you use them.
- The brain is an amazing part of the body especially when it comes to growth. With growth, the brain becomes strong and clever. When you learn new things, connections within the brain increase rapidly. Challenging yourself to grow only makes your brain cells grow which is what makes challenging tasks easy for you.
- Slips and fails happen but you need to tell yourself not to dwell on it or stay discouraged about it.

- If you're taking risks, the only thing you see may be setbacks and failures, so you may feel miserable. Don't dwell on it. You're not used to taking risks so your old mind will feel threatened and give you different cogent reasons to stop taking risks.
- When you protect yourself from others even if they aren't against you, you also hinder yourself from growth, prevent yourself from satisfying relationships, and get yourself ready for battle against the whole world.
- Sometimes children do too much to earn the love and admiration of their parents. When this happens, their goal isn't learning or development. It's about proving themselves to be worthy in the eyes of their parents.
- Your child isn't a mini version of you. Separate what you want from what your child needs.
- You can't improve or face your challenge without accepting that you have a challenge. Acceptance comes before change happens.

Goals

- To learn about mindset.
- To learn about the power of the brain.
- To understand why people hold onto a fixed mindset
- To understand why you need a mindset change.
- Understand why mindset change is difficult.
- To take risks
- To change from a fixed mindset to a growth mindset

- To be open to growth
- To hear your child in her actions and words
- To know how to change your fixed mindset.

Action plans

- Learning about mindset
- Learning about the power of the brain
- Understanding why people hold onto a fixed mindset.
- Understanding why you need a mindset change.
- Understanding why mindset change is difficult.
- Taking risks
- Changing from a fixed mindset to a growth mindset
- Becoming open to growth
- Hearing your child in her action and words
- Knowing how to change your fixed mindset.

Questions

1. Do you think change is easy? Explain the reason for your answer.
2. Why do people hold on to a fixed mindset?
3. Why shouldn't you be bothered about taking risks and growing?
4. Your friend applied for a job in one of the country's leading law firms because she was qualified for it. However, she didn't get the job. You know your friend has a fixed mindset. What can you tell her from a growth mindset to help her see things objectively?

5. Think about a decision you've been procrastinating about for a long time. Create a concrete plan to help you follow through with your decision and write it down.

6. As you begin to switch to becoming a more growth-minded person, what observations would you make from those around you and about yourself too?

7. Your nephew has a fixed mindset and you constantly see him comparing himself to others who don't have some of his talents. How can you help him? What can you say to him to help him adjust his mindset?

8. Why would it take a lot of growth mindset work to stay where a fixed mindset has always worked?

9. Your spouse has a problem controlling her temper. She realizes that she needs help, and she is creating strategies and plans to help her manage the situation. Join her to create a growth mindset self-control strategies and plans. Write them out. Ensure that you have a plan for setbacks as well.

As we wrap this up...

When we are born, we come into the world with the ability to learn. You'll notice this trait in babies and children. Intriguingly, many people forget this.

We are meant to keep learning through all the phases of our lives as long as we are here on earth. No one knows it all. And that's one thing you'll see in this book. You've got to love learning. As long as you're open to learning, you'll find out you're balanced and you'll have a naturally positive side to life. You don't need to fake it to make it.

This can only happen when you have the right mindset. There are two types of mindsets. They are the fixed mindset and the growth mindset.

Just like the name, a fixed mindset is one that's unchanging or fixed in its ways. It focuses on judgment and that's how it interprets the messages received. It makes an individual compare himself to others while feeling better than others. People with this mindset believe talent and skill are natural and they don't need to put in the effort to anything they do because it comes to them naturally. They see the world in black and white so it's either you are good or bad, you can change or you can't, relationships would work on their own or the relationship isn't meant to be.

Individuals with a growth mindset believe in learning and development. It's their perspective on life. This is a common trait in their friends, relationships, workplace, and everything around them. They constantly look for ways to improve and they put effort and determination into all they set out to do. They can learn skills and improve their skills when they set out to do anything.

Life comes with different curve balls and challenges, but with a growth mindset, things are not so difficult because you're focused on learning. With this mindset, you can be sure that you'll live a happy and satisfying life.

Made in United States
Troutdale, OR
08/16/2023

12126222R10044